Magnolia Scudieri
Director of the Museum

SAN MARCO

Complete Guide to the Museum
and Church

Scala Becocci

CONTENTS

3 Foreward

7 Introduction

11 Entrance Hall

14 Pilgrims' Hospice

44 Cloister of St Antonino

57 Lavatorium

60 Great Refectory

65 Fra Bartolomeo Room

68 Baldovinetti Room

73 The Dormitories

108 Library

115 Small Refectory

118 Foresteria

121 Cloister of the Silvestrine Monks

122 The Church of San Marco

© 1995 SCALA, Istituto Fotografico Editoriale, Antella
and Editrice Giusti di Becocci e C., Florence

Layout: Anthony Mathews
Text Layout: Sabina Carandini
Editing: Marilena Vecchi
Translation: Anthony Brierley
Photographs: SCALA ARCHIVE, except p. 95 below (Soprintendenza ai Beni Artistici e Storici)
Printed by: "Arti Grafiche" Stampa Nazionale, Calenzano (Florence), 1999

FOREWARD

If someone who had never been there were to ask me about the best way
to visit the Museum of San Marco, I would suggest that, before seeking out
the masterpieces of painting described in this guide and patiently going
through each part of the building and each room, the visitor should simply
let himself be guided by curiosity and wander around without any other
concern, than to drink in the absolutely unique atmosphere of the place.
In fact the visitor who expects to find here the kind of didactic and
historical system to which other museums of art in Italy and Europe have
accostumed us will be pleasently surprised, and perhaps somewhat
disconcerted. Once past the ticket office, the first thing you come to is a
harmonious cloister lined with frescos and dominated by a great cedar tree.
It is tempting (and something that I warmly recommand) to sit down here
on the low wall that runs round the cloister under the frescos that tell the
story of Bishop St Antonino, perhaps somewhere close to the Chapter
House where Fra Angelico gave such sublime form to his theological
reflections on the Crucifixion, and look around.
It is obvious at once that San Marco was an ideal place in which to live,
study and pray, a remarkable "City of God", set within the chaotic city of
men. It becomes clear, too, that Michelozzo and Fra Angelico, the two real
protagonists in the story of San Marco (the first because he was the
architect of the whole complex and the second because the museum is the
repository and emblem of his work), succeeded in creating, more than five
centuries ago, a relationship between humanity and art that no designer of
museums has ever been able to emulate.
Art is the fundamental means of human expression, an indispensable part of
our soul. It follows us, bringing order to our lives and offering us food for
thought. It cannot be forced down our throats but occupies an eloquent
and natural place as the backdrop to our daily lives. This is the idea that
inspired the founding of the Dominican monastery of San Marco and the
visitor to the public museum that it has become today, standing in any of
its rooms, will find this idea still perfectly comprehensible. This is why it is
worth, to begin with, wandering through the museum without following
any definite route, guided by the charm of the place itself, by the evocative
relationship between the art and the architecture, and by the immediately
apparent correspondence between the images and their symbolic function.
In this way we will pass through the shady refectories frescoed by
Ghirlandaio and Sogliani, the 'Ospizio' which once received pilgrims and
now houses some of Fra Angelico's greatest masterpieces, the 'Foresteria',
the cells on the upper floor, and the Library. Everywhere we are made

aware that the environment does justice to the art. The frescos, the painted panels, and the illuminated manuscripts communicate with us with an immediacy that would be inconceivable in any other museum.

Having grasped the magnificent uniqueness of San Marco, we are now ready to make use of the guide that Magnolia Scudieri – for many years a member of the museum staff – has written with loving care for Scala. Here we will learn that the museum houses some of the loftiest works of Western art, that Fra Angelico (the majority of whose work is here) is a great and unexpectedly modern painter, on a par with Masaccio and Piero della Francesca, and that the so-called school of San Marco (largely through the efforts of Fra Bartolomeo) represented one of the decisive turning points in the history of Italian art. We can learn much more from the museum with the help of this book , as long as we let ourselves be guided from the beginning (it is the easiest thing in the world) by the exceptional quality of this uniquely spiritual place.

Antonio Paolucci
Minister for Culture
and the Environment

The Museum of San Marco

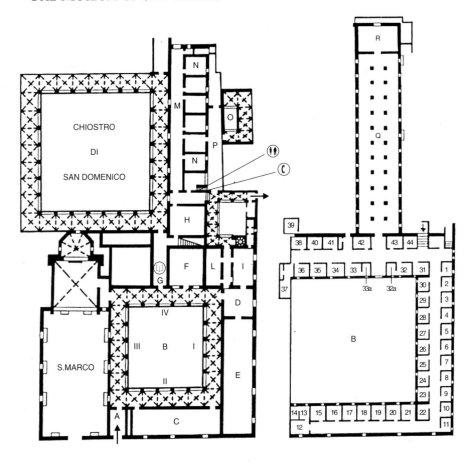

	GROUND FLOOR		
A	Entrance Hall	I	Fra Bartolomeo Room
B	Cloister of St Antonino	L	Baldovinetti Room
	(I, II, III, IV – sides of the cloister)	M-N	Foresteria
C	Pilgrims' Hospice	O	Cloister of the Silvestrine Monks
D	Lavatorium	P	Corte del Granaio
E	Great Refectory		
F	Chapter House		FIRST FLOOR
G	Corridor	Q	Library
H	Small Refectory	R	Greek Room
		1-43	Cells

Introduction

The Museum of San Marco is situated next to the church of the same name in the centre of Florence, not far from the Duomo, the Galleria dell'Accademia and other famous monuments and historic buildings. A number of factors make it unique among the city's museums. More than five hundred years from the time of its foundation, and in spite of numerous vicissitudes, the building has retained the original form of a Dominican monastery, whose functional purpose is still evident, a monastery which is the most distinguished living record of the historical and artistic achievements of the remarkable people who lived here, from St Antonino to Fra Girolamo Savonarola, Fra Angelico and Fra Bartolomeo. The Museum comprises the oldest nucleus of the Dominican monastery which Michelozzo, the Medici's favourite architect, rebuilt in a single decade between about 1436 and 1446. Michelozzo carried out the project on the orders and at the total expense of Cosimo il Vecchio, using as a foundation the older monastery of the Silvestrine monks who had been exiled to San Giorgio alla Costa. At around the same time Fra Giovanni Angelico, one of the leading painters of the Renaissance, frescoed it for his Dominican brothers.

Michelozzo's monastery of San Marco was built on a higher level than the original building, although some of the still solid older walls were incorporated into the new larger construction. The survival of some of these earlier structures has been proved by the recent finds of fragments of 14th-century mural painting under the floor of some of the cells. The design was modern and functional, as can still be appreciated from the organized layout of the various rooms.

The result is a complex of monumental proportions, organized rationally and responding to all the needs of a large religious community. The monastery was enriched with an extraordinary cycle of paintings by Fra Angelico which decorate the cells, the corridors, the cloister and the chapter house. These paintings, today incredibly conserved in their entirety, were linked symbolically to the places of single and collective religious meditation and adherence to the Dominican rule. On the ground floor, around the large cloister dedicated to St Antonino (prior at the time of the monastery's reconstruction, he became archbishop of Florence in 1446, and his stories were illustrated in the frescoed lunettes on the walls in the course of the 17th century), are the rooms dedicated to the communal life of the friars: the Pilgrims' Hospice near the entrance, the Chapter House frescoed by Angelico, the Lavatorium and Great Refectory frescoed in the 16th century by Giovanni Antonio Sogliani, and the adjacent areas, today used as exhibition rooms, which were formerly used as kitchens and service rooms, including another small 15th-century cloister, the Chiostro della Spesa, and a courtyard, the Corte del Granaio. A vestibule adjoining the Cloister of St Antonino gives access to the stairs leading to the dormitories and Library on the floor above. At the foot of the stairs, on the right for those descending them, is the Small Refectory, containing Ghirlandaio's late 15th-century fresco of the *Last Supper*, and the old Foresteria, or guest-quarters. These rooms all give onto the second large cloister, which was begun by Michelozzo, finished in the 16th century, and several times restored, with 18th-century frescoes depicting the Stories of St Dominic. Later extensions of the monastic complex have grown up around it and are today used by the Dominican fathers. Here Giorgio La Pira, another key figure in the spiritual and civil history of Florence who was closely associated with the Dominican community and culture, had his headquarters and meditative refuge in the 1950s.

If the sobriety and elegance of Florentine Renaissance architecture are immediately visible in the first cloister, the height of intellectual virtuosity which it reached can be seen in the Library, the first Renaissance library to be open to the public. Cosimo donated to the Library a precious collection of Italian, Latin and Greek manuscripts once belonging to the humanist Niccolò Niccoli (these are now housed in the Biblioteca Medicea Laurenziana). The Library today houses a fine collection of over a hundred medieval and Renaissance illuminated choirbooks coming from this and other suppressed monasteries.

On the first floor the fascination of the place increases with the marriage between the extraordinary intellectualistic clearness of the basilical structure of the Library, a temple of knowledge, and the mystical clearness of the rhythmic grey-white division of the corridors' long walls, where the arched ribbing of the cell doors seems to be multiplied infinitely from penumbra towards the light of the windows at the end, real light which becomes as unreal as the light given off and radiated by the frescoes in every cell.

Our visit of the Museum proceeds thus, moving from one room to another, following an ancient pattern of monastic life that is relived in images which seem to shut out the bustle of city life outside the walls. The Museum is also unique for the natural relationship, now rarely found, between the container and its contents, between the building and the works in it, and the existence of a historical guiding thread that links the building, the historical figures associated with it and the works of art conserved in it today, even when these have come from different original locations.

Founded in 1869, following the government's suppression of the monasteries in 1866, the Museum, now a national monument, set out in true Risorgimento spirit to be primarily a monument to Dominican and city history together, by exploiting both the artistic legacy – Angelico's frescoes in the cells and those by Fra Bartolomeo, which monastic seclusion had made inaccessible to the public – and the historical legacy left here by the passage of Savonarola and St Antonino. From 1891 Guido Carocci, then keeper of the Museum, tenaciously pursued this objective, seeking to enrich the Museum as much as he could by accumulating here other works by Angelico and Fra Bartolomeo, as well as those by other artists associated with Dominican history. This objective – at least as regards the Monographic Museum of Angelico – was realized only in 1921 with the transfer here of almost all Angelico's works on wood in the possession of the Florentine galleries. Carocci also cultivated what he always considered was the Museum's secondary function, that is, as a container for the decorative, sculptural and architectural fragments saved from the demolition of the former city centre which was begun in 1881. The pieces, which started to arrive from 1894 onwards, formed a special section, "The Museum of Old Florence", inaugurated in 1898 and later enlarged. This was situated in the Foresteria – where it still is today – and in the Cloister of St Dominic, from where it was moved to the restored cellars twenty years ago.

Over the last ten years, in addition to the value attached to Angelico's works (undoubtedly the most important part of the Museum) through the restoration of all the frescoes and a new exhibition of all his works on wood in the Pilgrims' Hospice, efforts have been made to salvage other old rooms like the kitchens and sculleries, which over the years had been misused and neglected, and, with the exhibition of other works, to enrich the historical and artistic heritage represented by the religious institution and the artists who had left their mark here. The Baldovinetti Room was created to house works by followers of Angelico or artists influenced by him, and another room was dedicated to Fra Bartolomeo, the second important painter and Dominican friar who lived and worked at San Marco at the beginning of the 16th century, the faithful interpreter of the devotional and didactic conception of art advanced by Savonarola. Savonarola, indissolubly linked to the history of the monastery, of which he was prior, was captured by his enemies in 1498 and burnt at the stake in Piazza Signoria, as is documented in two contemporary paintings displayed in his cells on the first floor together with his relics.

The Great Refectory is dominated by the *Miraculous Supper of St Dominic*, painted in 1536 by Giovanni Antonio Sogliani, heir of the devotional tradition started by Fra Bartolomeo. In this room, paintings of the 16th-18th centuries have been displayed which reflect the development of this figurative tradition in the decoration of monasteries.

The two large cloisters already mentioned, the Cloister of St Antonino and the Cloister of St Dominic (today used by the Dominican monks and only partially included in the Museum's itinerary and accessible to the public), are the setting for two great painting cycles representing the lives of the two saints. They are complete examples (then common, but rarely surviving) of the painting of religious history. One was frescoed from the very first years of the 17th century by the most famous fresco painters of the time – Bernardino Poccetti, Fabrizio Boschi, Giovan Battista Vanni, Matteo Rosselli and others; the other was painted at the beginning of the 18th century by Alessandro Gherardini, Sebastiano Galeotti, Cosimo Ulivelli and others. The frescoes, which are in a somewhat precarious condition, are presently being restored. It is hoped, therefore, that we shall soon be able to enjoy the frequent glimpses of Tuscan countryside and views of the city's single monuments which are often the only visual document of their existence.

Entrance Hall

We enter the Museum through a narrow vestibule dominated by two imposing 18th-century tomb monuments situated on the side walls – the one on the left late-Baroque, the one on the right pre-neoclassical. A further note of austerity is added by the presence of various 19th-century tombstones, the only ones surviving *in loco* after the total removal, in 1970-72, of those in the Cloister of St Antonino, which are today housed in the underground Lapidarium (visitable by arrangement).

Unknown 18th-Century Sculptor
Funerary Monument of Roberto degli Ubaldini da Gagliano
350x270 cm, marble

The monument was erected on the wishes of its subject in 1714, one year before his death. The celebratory intent, openly declared in the inscription of the elegant plaque in which the deceased wanted many of his official charges mentioned, is also clearly manifested in the typology of the monument, an example of refined late-Baroque virtuosity, the pomposity of the composition, the chromatic and material richness of the marbles and the attitude of the figure emerging from the niche.

Proceeding through a gate, we walk into one of the architectural jewels of the Florentine Renaissance – the great 15th-century Cloister of St Antonino, its harmonious arches resting on columns with classical Ionic capitals. The windows of the dormitory cells built by Michelozzo look onto the cloister, and all the various parts of the monastery are arranged around it. At the same time the visitor's eye is caught by the painting of *Christ on the Cross Adored by St Dominic* on the end wall of the first side of the cloister, the first fresco painted by Fra Angelico to be seen in the Museum which introduces us to the mystical atmosphere and artistic tension of the monastic complex.

Before approaching the fresco and completing the round of the cloister, a visit to the old Pilgrims' Hospice situated to the right is recommended.

Pilgrims' Hospice

This monumental room is situated in the perimeter defined by the original medieval structure which in the 15th century Michelozzo raised and covered with cross vaults to support the dormitories above. Today it houses the Museum's art gallery of works by Fra Angelico, that is, the collection of works painted by Angelico and his assistants for churches and monasteries in Florence and the surrounding area, which were transferred to the Florentine galleries following the suppression of the religious guilds in 1866 and which came to San Marco in 1919. The creation of the Angelico Monographic Museum completed the original project of dedicating this institution to the history of the Dominican faith and therefore to those figures who had contributed to the culture, faith and art of the order.

Guido di Piero was born in Vicchio di Mugello around 1395. He was a painter in 1417, and joined the Dominican Order with the name Fra Giovanni before 1423. For some years he lived in San Domenico near Fiesole among observers of the reform of Giovanni Dominici before coming to San Marco to undertake the decoration of the monastery on the commission of the Medici family. Throughout his life he married his religious commitment with a feverish activity as a painter and illuminator of manuscripts. Keenly aware of the cultural revolution taking place at this time, he was able to channel the various expressions of it in the context of a devoutly religious vision which from the 15th century earned him the name "Angelico" and made him one of the central figures of the early Florentine Renaissance.

FRA ANGELICO (c 1395 – 1455)
and LORENZO MONACO (c 1370 – 1423)
Deposition
In the cusps: *'Noli me tangere', Resurrection, Maries at the Sepulchre*
In the pilasters (from left): *Saints John the Baptist, Anthony Abbot, Lawrence, Benedict, Michael, Francis, Andrew, Giovanni Gualberto, Peter, Peter Martyr, Paul, Dominic, Stephen, a bearded saint, Augustine and Jerome*
At the top: *St John, a prophet, David, a prophet*
185x176 cm, wood, inv. 1890 no. 8509

The altarpiece was commissioned for the sacristy of Santa Trinita by Palla Strozzi, whose family was the patron of that church. It was initially entrusted to Lorenzo Monaco who executed the scenes in the cusps and three predella panels which are now at the Galleria dell'Accademia. The painting was left unfinished at his death in 1425 and was completed by Fra Angelico in the 1530s. Angelico overcame the problem of the painting's tripartite division (imposed by the arches) by creating a spatial composition in the form of an X with the fulcrum in the central cross, thus fulfilling the requirements of an open, perspective space. Behind the three groups of figures that populate the scene, which according to Vasari includes a portrait of Michelozzo (the man in the black hat), a receding landscape depicts hills, towns and castles typical of the Tuscan countryside.

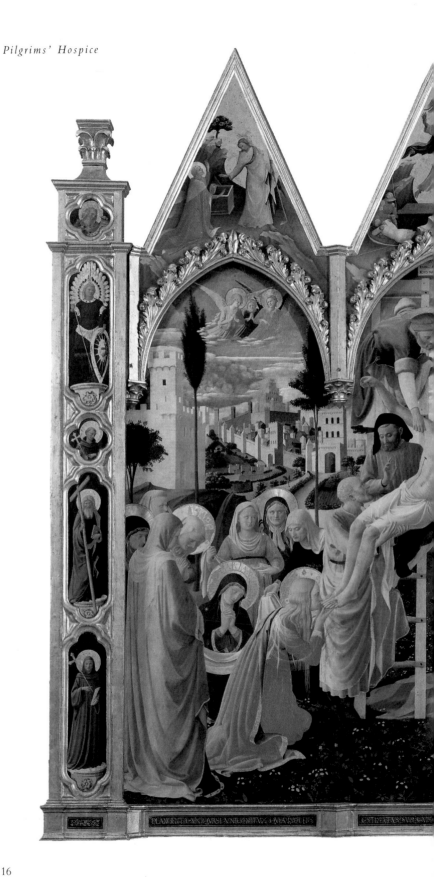

17

FRA ANGELICO (c 1395 – 1455)
Triptych of St Peter Martyr
Madonna and Child with Saints Dominic, John the Baptist, Peter Martyr
and Thomas Aquinas
In the cusps: *Annunciation, God the Father.* Between the cusps: *Preaching and*
*Martyrdom of St Pete*r
137x168 cm, wood, inv. 1890 no. 8769

This painting was certainly executed before 1429, the year of a document
recording that payment still had to be made for it by the nuns of San Pietro
Martire to the monastery of San Domenico at Fiesole, where Angelico resided at
the time. The early dating, which makes it the first work that can certainly be
attributed to Angelico, is also confirmed by the still Gothic conception of the
work, in which the rather static figures are slightly turned and thus seen in three-
quarter profiles, a tentative hint at three-dimensionality. The stories in the cusps
have greater freedom and fluency, showing that Angelico was familiar with the
technique of manuscript illumination, an art he had practised in his youth.

F R A   A N G E L I C O
The Naming of John the Baptist
26x24 cm, wood, inv. 1890 no. 1499

It has been suggested that this panel, together with the one of *St James Freeing Hermogenes* of the Fort Worth Museum in Texas and others recently identified, belonged to a dismantled predella, perhaps that of the *Annunciation* of the Prado. Although it has exquisite touches of late-Gothic art, the painting, with its accurate rendering of the Michelozzian architecture in the background and the new spatial relationships between the figures and between the figures and their setting, shows that Masaccio's teaching has been fully assimilated.
The work can be dated shortly before 1435, the year in which Andrea di Giusto copied it for his polyptych in the Pinacoteca di Prato.

FRA ANGELICO (c 1395 – 1455)
Marriage of the Virgin
Funeral of the Virgin
19x50 cm, 19x51 cm, wood, inv. 1890 nos. 1493–1501

The two small panels are thought to be part of the predella with the *Coronation of the Virgin* of Santa Maria Nuova, now at the Uffizi, datable to 1434–35. The

works, which at first sight appear to be virtuous expressions of colour and line, are actually well-measured spatial constructions that are purely Renaissance in character. In the *Marriage*, the artist seems to extend the limited physical space defined by the horizontal form of the panel by arranging the figures against the oblique planes of the architectural structures. In the *Funeral,* he gives the scene depth with the simple device of the symmetrical, heavily slanting lines of perspective created by the figures and rocks.

FRA ANGELICO (c 1395 - 1455)
Last Judgement
105x210 cm, wood, inv. 1890 no. 8505

The painting was probably commissioned around 1431 for the church of Santa
Maria degli Angeli, when Ambrogio Traversari, who gave a significant impetus to
the church's renewal, was elected abbot general of the Camaldolensian Order. It is
probable that the work was originally intended for the decoration of the upper

part of the choristers' seat backs. With a daring pyramidal composition Angelico superseded the medieval iconographical tradition which usually structured the Judgement in levels one above the other, and acknowledged the new need to adapt the image to a real space. He therefore balanced the sphere of the Elect and the sphere of the Damned with the ingenious insertion of the central line of uncovered tombs receding into the distance. In embracing these new tendencies, however, the artist did not renounce his lyrical, decorative style, as can be seen in the dance of the Blessed.

FRA ANGELICO (c 1395 - 1455)
and ALESSO BALDOVINETTI (1425 - 1499)
Doors of the Silver Cabinet

The panels, today assembled in four groups, with thirty-five stories from the
Gospels, bordered by two scrolls with verses from the Old and New Testaments,
were originally part of the door of the silver and ex-voto cabinet in the Basilica of
Santissima Annunziata. The cabinet was removed from its original location as early
as the 17th century and taken apart in the 18th century, thus surviving in a
dismantled state. Fra Angelico, who started work on it around 1450, was
responsible for most of the execution immediately carrying out the first nine

A FRA ANGELICO
Mystic Wheel, Annunciation, Nativity, Circumcision, Adoration of the Magi,
Presentation in the Temple, Flight into Egypt, Massacre of the Innocents, Christ
Teaching in the Temple
123x123 cm, wood, inv. 1890 nos. 8489, 8490, 8491

panels, but leaving the later completion of those remaining to various assistants, including Alesso Baldovinetti. In 1461 the cabinet was altered by the addition of six more panels, now lost, painted by Piero del Massaio. In these stories, which are characterized by a certain complexity, the artist faithfully reproduced the architectural settings and compositional forms already experimented in his large-scale works.

B ALESSO BALDOVINETTI
Marriage at Cana, Baptism of Christ, Transfiguration
123x44 cm, wood, inv. 1890 no. 8510

Following page

C FRA ANGELICO
Raising of Lazarus, Entry into Jerusalem, Last Supper, Betrayal of Judas, Washing of the Disciples' Feet, Communion of the Apostles, Agony in the Garden, Kiss of Judas, Arrest of Christ, Christ before Caiphas, Mocking of Christ, Flagellation
123x160 cm, wood, inv. 1890 nos. 8492, 8500

D FRA ANGELICO
Ascent to Calvary, Christ Stripped of his Garments, Crucifixion, Lamentation over the Dead Christ, Christ in Limbo, Three Maries at the Sepulchre, Ascension, Pentecost, Last Judgement, Coronation of the Virgin, "Lex Amoris"
123x160 cm, wood, inv. 1890 nos. 8501, 8502

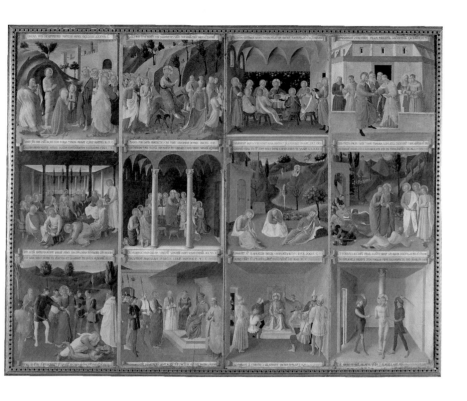

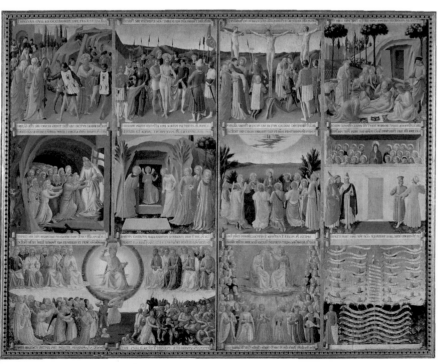

FRA ANGELICO (c 1395 - 1455)
Tabernacles of Santa Maria Novella

The first, known as the "Madonna of the Star", is the most famous of the four tabernacles which sources inform us were commissioned by Fra Giovanni Masi for Santa Maria Novella, the mother church of the Dominicans. Three of these are now housed in the Museum of San Marco; the remaining one is in the Stewart Gardner Museum in Boston.

Madonna and Child, God the Father, Angels
In the predella: *Saints Peter Martyr, Dominic and Thomas Aquinas*
84x51 cm, wood, San Marco inv. no. 274

Annunciation and *Adoration of the Magi*
In the predella: *Madonna and Child with Saints Catherine of Siena, Apollonia, Margaret, Lucy, Mary Magdalen, Catherine of Alexandria, Agnes, Cecilia, Dorothea and Ursula*
84x50 cm, wood, San Marco inv. no. 276

Probably executed shortly before the death of Masi in 1434, the works reflect the variety of cultural references which the art of Angelico expressed at the time. In the first, the rounded figure of the Virgin reminds us of Masaccio, the movement of the drapery recalls Ghiberti and the Holy Child's gesture is reminiscent of Donatello. In the second, with the *Adoration of the Magi,* we see evidence of the soft line characteristic of Masolino and of Gothic illuminated manuscripts north of the Alps. In the third, with the *Coronation of the Virgin,* there is already that search for monumentality and precise spatial definition which would be definitively expressed a few years later in the large work of the same subject, today at the Louvre.

Coronation of the Virgin
In the predella: *Adoration of the Child and Angels*
69x37 cm, wood, San Marco inv. no. 275

F R A   A N G E L I C O   (c 1395 – 1455)
Madonna and Child and the Holy Trinity
190x81 cm, wood, inv. 1890 no. 8496

This painting, whose original location is unknown, has been identified as the central part of a dismantled triptych, possibly one of the two which sources record were executed for the Carthusian monastery of Galluzzo. Two other panels at the Museum whose frames match this one, with Saints Jerome, John the Baptist, Francis and Honofrius, and the Annunciation, may be the side panels of the same work. The clear spatial definition of the figures, combined with the fine colour and line, suggest that the work was executed in the 1420s, at the end of the artist's youthful period when his new Renaissance vision was beginning to take form.

FRA ANGELICO (c 1395 – 1455)
Lamentation over the Dead Christ
105x164 cm, wood, inv. 1890 no. 8487

The panel was commissioned in 1436 by Fra Sebastiano Benintendi, who may be portrayed here in the guise of St Dominic. Benintendi was the nephew of the blessed Villana delle Botti whom we see depicted beside St Catherine. The work seems to have been completed in 1441, a date which appears in the hem of the Virgin's cloak. It was an extreme image for those who, condemned to death, spent the last hours of their lives in that oratory. In Angelico's treatment of this popular medieval theme, the undulating horizontal rhythm of the composition moves away from the figures into space, is taken up again in the arm of the cross at the top of the painting and in the background by the walls of Jerusalem, a rhythm that dissolves the drama of the event into the quiet awareness of future hope. The painting was damaged at the bottom during floods when it was in the oratory near the Arno river.

ZANOBI STROZZI (1412 – 1468)
Madonna and Child Enthroned with Four Angels
127x110 cm, wood, inv. 1890 no. 3204

The panel, originally from Santa Maria Nuova, is one of the few works which almost all critics agree in attributing to Zanobi Strozzi, an artist heavily influenced by Fra Angelico (as this painting, reminiscent of the *Linaioli Tabernacle*, reveals) whose activity has often been mistaken for that of his master. Zanobi Strozzi's only documented works, in the field of manuscript illumination, do in fact show other cultural influences besides those of Angelico which if studied more closely might lead to a more accurate identification of his art.

FRA ANGELICO (c 1395 – 1455)
Linaioli Tabernacle
Madonna and Child Enthroned

On the exterior of the door panels: *St Mark and St Peter*. On the interior of the
door panels: *St John the Baptist and St Mark*. In the predella: *St Peter Preaching before
St Mark, Adoration of the Magi, Martyrdom of St Mark*
292x176 cm (closed); 39x56 cm (each panel of the predella), wood,
inv. 1890 no. 879

This large tabernacle was commissioned in 1433 by the Arte dei Linaioli (Linen Guild), at whose premises it remained until 1777. It was the first great public work executed by the artist and the first time he had tackled such large dimensions. This work marks the end of Angelico's early period and the beginning of his mature work. In the Madonna the artist draws on the figurative tradition of past masters, Lorenzo Monaco and Gentile da Fabriano, and combines it with an awareness of the physicalness of bodies and the arrangement of figures in space which he had acquired from Masaccio. In the statuesque angels, and more so in the saints, we can see the influence of Ghiberti and Luca della Robbia. The narrative dimension is developed in the predella where the artist shows a particular interest in architecture, an architecture, however, still conceived as a scenic background rather than as a real setting. The marble frame was designed by Ghiberti and executed by his assistants Jacopo di Bartolomeo and Simone di Nanni.

ASSISTANT OF FRA ANGELICO
(first half of the 15th century)
'Vir dolorum' and Adoration of the Magi
97x54 cm, wood, inv. 1890 no. 8499

The subjects of the two scenes painted on the panel, originally from the
monastery of San Domenico, recall the iconography adopted by Angelico in
various paintings such as the frescoes of cells 27 and 28 (the first) and in the
predella of the Montecarlo altarpiece (the second). The style, however,
characterized by a rougher and more rigid line, suggests that the painting was the
work of an as yet unidentified assistant.

FRA ANGELICO (c 1395 - 1455)
Bosco ai Frati Altarpiece
Madonna and Child Enthroned with Saints Anthony of Padua, Louis of Toulouse, Francis, Cosmas, Damian and Peter Martyr
In the predella: *Ecce Homo with Saints Dominic, Bernardine, Peter, Paul, Jerome and Benedict*
174x174 cm, 26x174 cm (predella), wood, inv. 1890 nos. 8503-8507

The presence of the Medici saints Cosmas and Damian is one of the elements suggesting that this work was ordered by Cosimo de' Medici, who in 1438 had already commissioned Michelozzo to rebuild the church of the monastery of San Bonaventura al Bosco ai Frati in the Mugello. Although damaged at the sides, this altarpiece retains its monumental aspect due to the richness of the architectural setting. This classical opulence, which some critics have called pre-Bramante in style, is typical of Angelico's Roman works. This characteristic dates the work after 1450, as does the presence of St Bernardine, who was in fact canonized in 1450.

F R A   A N G E L I C O   (c 1395 - 1455)
Crucifixion
Coronation of the Virgin
28x28,3 cm, wood, inv. 1890 nos. 8497 and 8498

The two circular panels, perhaps originally part of a reliquary, are believed (not unanimously) to be by Angelico, since they are similar to other compositions of a similar subject painted in the cells. They are distinguished from these by an emphasis on line and a range of intense colours which suggest that they date from the artist's youthful period. The panels come from the church of the Croce al Tempio whence they were transferred to the Confraternita of Santa Lucia in Santissima Annunziata.

FRA ANGELICO
San Marco Altarpiece
Madonna and Child Enthroned with Angels and Saints Cosmas, Damian, Lawrence, John the Evangelist, Mark, Dominic, Francis and Peter Martyr
In the predella: *Burial of Cosmas and Damian with their Brothers; Healing of the Deacon Justinian* (illustrations at page 42)
220x227 cm; 37x45 cm (each panel of the predella), wood, inv. 1890 nos. 8506, 8494, 8495

This altarpiece was painted between 1438 and 1443 for the new high altar in the church of San Marco, restored together with the monastery by Michelozzo at the behest of the Medici Family and consecrated by Pope Eugenius IV. It replaced the triptych by Lorenzo di Niccolò which was moved to the church of San Domenico in Cortona.

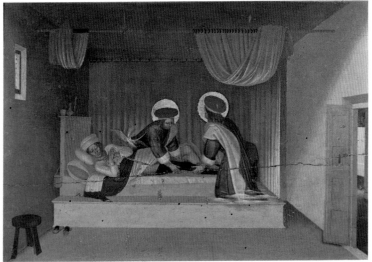

There is no compositional division in this 'Sacra conversazione', but a unity in the precise and monumental system of perspective which places the holy group in the centre and at a distance. The illusionary device of a simulated tabernacle with a crucifixion in the foreground alludes to the holy group. The painting can be said to be a prototype of the 15th-century Florentine altarpiece. Characterized by order, symmetry, classicism and the importance of a natural-looking landscape, the work conforms to the new Renaissance vision, and despite damage caused by soda in a previous restoration, the painting still succeeds in getting across its innovating message. Of the nine panels forming the predella only two are kept in the Museum of San Marco. In one panel we see the monastery of San Marco during Michelozzo's renovation and in the other a glimpse of an interior furnished in the style of the time. The remaining panels are in museums in Washington, Munich, Dublin and Paris.

FRA ANGELICO (c 1395 - 1455)
Annalena Altarpiece
Madonna and Child Enthroned with Saints Peter Martyr, Cosmas, Damian,
John the Evangelist, Lawrence and Francis
In the predella: *Healing of Palladia, Cosmas and Damian before Lycias, Cosmas*
and Damian Saved from Drowning, Attempt to Kill Cosmas and Damian by
Burning, Attempt to Kill Cosmas and Damian by Crucifying and Stoning,
Beheading of Cosmas and Damian
180x202 cm, wood, inv. 1890 nos. 8493, 8486

Once in the Florentine monastery of Annalena which took its name from
Annalena Malatesta, the spiritual daughter of St Antonino who founded it in
1453, this work has always been considered as pre-dating the San Marco
altarpiece and as having been painted between 1434 and 1440. Recently,
however, it has been suggested that the work was painted at a later date,
subsequent to the founding of the monastery. The predella, in fact, which
appears to be the work of assistants and copies some themes from the
predella of the San Marco altarpiece by the master himself, must have been
painted after and not before the work for San Marco. The architecture in
the background, moreover, looks Roman rather than Michelozzian and
therefore more similar to the Bosco ai Frati altarpiece. The Annalena
altarpiece can therefore be dated after 1450.

CLOISTER OF ST ANTONINO

After leaving the Pilgrims' Hospice, the visitor is advised to continue along
the right side of the cloister as far as the entrance to the Lavatorium, then go
back to the entrance in order to complete the entire circuit. In this way the
visitor can enjoy a view of the campanile – executed in 1512 on a design by
Baccio d'Agnolo – and the two-light Gothic windows on the side of the
church, and will be able to follow in their chronological sequence the
lunettes frescoed with the Stories of St Antonino, whose subjects are
described below the scenes. St Antonino was responsible for the coming of
the Dominicans to San Marco and was prior at the time of the monastery's
reconstruction. The painting of the cycle celebrating his life was started by
Bernardino Poccetti in 1602, proceeded after the latter's death with the
contributions of various other important painters and was completed in 1626
by Matteo Rosselli. In 1693 Pier Dandini added another two episodes in the
lunette splays near the Chapter House.
In 1629 Cecco Bravo was commissioned to fill with the *Mourners* the empty
space around *Christ on the Cross Adored by St Dominic*, painted by Fra
Angelico. In 1652 the small lunettes above the doors painted by Angelico
with subjects alluding to religious daily life in the various parts of the
monastery were framed with allegorical figures by Giovan Battista Vanni.

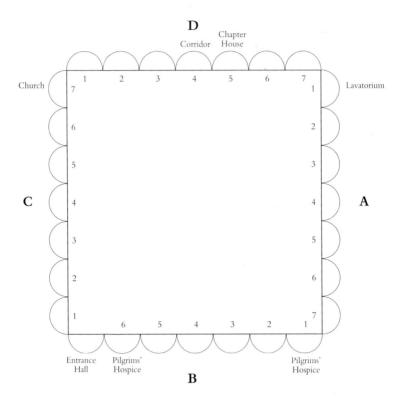

SIDE A
1. Fra Angelico *Pietà;* Giovan Battista Vanni *Charity and Justice*
2. Bernardino Poccetti *The young Antonino Adoring the Cross of Orsanmichele*
3. Bernardino Poccetti *Antonino Becomes a Dominican Monk*
4. Lodovico Buti *St Antonino Brings a Boy Back to Life*
5. Alessandro Tiarini *St Antonino's Prediction to a Merchant*
6. Alessandro Tiarini *St Antonino Witnesses the Restoration of San Marco*
7. Alessandro Tiarini *Pope Eugenius IV Consecrates the Church of San Marco*

SIDE B
1. Fra Angelico *Christ Received by Two Dominicans;* Giovan Battista Vanni *Angels*
2. Bernardino Poccetti *St Antonino Becomes Bishop of Florence*
3. Lorenzo Cerrini *The Preaching of St Antonino*
4. Bernardino Poccetti (attr. to) *St Antonino Saves the Canon Machiavelli from Drowning*
5. Michele Cinganelli *St Antonino Institutes the Confraternita de' Buonomini*
6. Fra Angelico *St Thomas Aquinas;* Giovan Battista Vanni *The Miracle of the Key in the Fish's Belly*

SIDE C
1. Fabrizio Boschi *St Antonino Banishes Onlookers from a Newly-Wed Bride*
2. Bernardino Poccetti *St Antonino Saves Two Youths from Drowning*
3. Bernardino Poccetti *St Antonino Cools Metal in an Ironworks*
4. Lorenzo Cerrini *St Antonino Absolves the Magistrates of the 'Otto di Balia'*
5. Sigismondo Coccapani *St Antonino Castigates Two Blindmen Feigning Poverty*
6. Fabrizio Boschi *St Antonino Overturns a Gambling-Table*
7. Fra Angelico *St Peter Martyr Calls for Silence;* Giovan Battista Vanni *Faith and Hope*

SIDE D
1. Fra Angelico *Christ on the Cross Adored by St Dominic ;* Cecco Bravo *Mourners and Angels*
2. Bernardino Poccetti *St Antonino on a Papal Mission*
3. Bernardino Poccetti *The Miracle of Fertility*
4. Pier Dandini *St Antonino Administers Spiritual Aid to Plague Victims*
5. Fra Angelico *St Dominic with the Discipline and the Rule*
6. Pier Dandini *St Antonino Talks with a Greedy Farmer*
7. Matteo Rosselli *The Death of St Antonino*

FRA ANGELICO (c 1395 - 1455)
Pietà
120x127 cm, detached fresco

GIOVAN BATTISTA VANNI (1600 - 1660)
Charity and Justice
234x410 cm, detached fresco

Like the other frescoes of the cloister Fra Angelico's lunette was painted around
1440-42. Its extreme essentiality gives it an intense emotional force, although it
does appear rather suffocated by the exuberant figures of *Virtues* and *Putti* painted
at the sides with typical Baroque emphasis by Vanni, a painter influenced by
Pietro da Cortona. Angelico's image, alluding to the Resurrection and therefore
to that eternal life which is attainable through feeding on Christ's body, acted as a
reminder for the monks, who through that door entered the Refectory for their
earthly sustenance.

BERNARDINO BARBATELLI called IL POCCETTI
(1548 - 1612)
The Young Antonino Adoring the Cross of Orsanmichele
234x440 cm, fresco

This lunette is the first work in the cycle of frescoes celebrating the life and miracles of St Antonino, prior of the monastery from 1439 to 1444 and bishop of Florence from 1446 to 1455, who was canonized in 1523. The cycle of paintings was financed by various Florentine noble families, whose coats of arms are placed in the middle of the inscriptions beneath the frescoes. The lunette, like the one adjacent to it (signed), was executed in 1602 or shortly after by Poccetti, a popular artist who was extremely active in the decoration of cloisters, and probably masterminded the entire cycle, which he conducted with the help of assistants until his death. The grandiose architectural setting (note the still open loggias of Orsanmichele), the lively colours and the accomplished draughtsmanship make it one of the artist's finest achievements.

STEFANO RICCI (1765 - 1837)
Monument to Giovan Cosimo degli Alessandri
280x163 cm, marble

This monument was raised to the memory of the Curator of the Royal Statues Gallery, who died in 1828, and who won recognition for his opposition to the French forces who were intent on demolishing the church and monastery to make a field for military exercises. Purely neoclassical in its archeological references, it is one of the finest monuments among those situated along the walls of the cloister in honour of illustrious citizens who had earned particular distinction in the field of culture. The sculptor, a pupil of Francesco Carradori, and president of the Florentine Academy, was a leading artist of the Florentine neoclassical movement.

ALESSANDRO TIARINI (1577 - 1668)
St Antonino Witnesses the Restoration of San Marco
230x440 cm, fresco

This lunette, together with the ones before and after, represents the debut in Tuscany of this late-Mannerist Bolognese painter who stayed in Florence between 1599 and 1606.
Tiarini was an apprentice in the workshop of Domenico Passignano, whose influence is evident in the intense colours. In this work, the devotional tone and deeply expressive portraits show that the artist has absorbed various aspects of the "reformed" Florentine painting. Among the bystanders on the right are Cosimo the Elder, Lorenzo de' Medici, St Antonino and possibly Michelozzo.

BERNARDINO BARBATELLI called IL POCCETTI (1548-1612)
St Antonino Becomes Bishop of Florence
230x412 cm, fresco

This is another example of the theatrical vision typical of Poccetti's compositions. First trained in grotesque decoration, Poccetti was Buontalenti's assistant in his scenographic and architectural studies, then a prolific painter of frescoes; he was responsible for cycles of paintings on both religious and profane themes in the most important cloisters and palaces of Florence. The most interesting element in this fresco, in addition to the anachronistic inclusion of Savonarola and his followers as bystanders in the scene – a reference to the works of Fra Bartolomeo – is the view of the cathedral facade before its demolition in 1587. Here, on the side buttress, we still see the enormous terracotta statue of Joshua made by Donatello between 1410 and 1412.

FABRIZIO BOSCHI (1572 – 1642)
St Antonino Banishes Onlookers from a Newly-Wed Bride
230x410 cm, fresco

This is one of two lunettes which the artist painted on the wall. Returning from a
stay in Rome between 1602 and 1606, where he had an early opportunity to
become acquainted with the painting of Rubens, Boschi inserts into the usual
Poccetti-style narrative tone a new monumentality in the figures, at that time
unknown in Florentine art. The painting, alas, has suffered heavy damage in the
course of the centuries.

UNKNOWN 18TH-
CENTURY SCULPTOR
**Monument to Anton Francesco
Gori**
229x145 cm, marble

The monument was executed in 1757
at the death of Gori, and bears the
epitaph which the deceased himself
had composed. It combines the
classical sobriety of the aedicula with
the realistic vivacity of the bust
portrait, and is of interest above all for
its commemoration of the dead man,
an eminent scholar, a man of letters
and religion, a historian, an
empassioned connoisseur and collector
of Etruscan antiquities, and author in
1728 of a detailed description of the
construction of the Salviati Chapel in
the church of San Marco and the
transfer of St Antonino's body .

S I G I S M O N D O   C O C C A P A N I   (1583 - 1643)
St Antonino Castigates Two Blindmen Feigning Poverty
237x432 cm, fresco

This is the first known work by this gifted artist who was also a man of letters, architecture and science, the author of a treatise on the regulation of the waters of the River Arno. He painted the fresco on his return to Florence after a long stay in Rome with his master Cigoli. Rome was at that time the centre of the artistic avant-garde and Coccapani stayed there in the stimulating company of different artists, such as Fetti, the followers of Caravaggio and Pomarancio, whose influence can be seen in this lunette. The Tuscan setting is illuminated by the vibrant Venetian-style light, drapes and colours and has a touch of a certain kind of genre painting.

F R A   A N G E L I C O (c 1395 - 1455)
Christ on the Cross Adored by St Dominic
340x206 cm, fresco

F R A N C E S C O   M O N T E L A T I C I called C E C C O   B R A V O
(1601 - 1661)
Mourners and Angels
413x86 cm each, detached frescoes

The beautiful Crucifixion, the first of a series of similar works executed in the dormitories, was probably made at the same time as the great *Crucifixion* in the Chapter House which was completed in 1442. The monumentality of Christ's body, anatomically thrown into relief by the light, and the vivid expression of St Dominic, two figures standing starkly against a bare and unreal background, are a synthesis of the artistic and spiritual message, in the context of Renaissance realism, typical of Angelico's art. In 1628, when the Fabbroni family was given permission to build a tomb here, the fresco was surrounded by a marble frame and flanked by the *Mourners* painted by the young Cecco Bravo, a pupil of Giovanni Bilivert and Matteo Rosselli.

FLORENTINE ART OF THE 15TH CENTURY
Bell
120x110 cm, bronze, San Marco inv. no. 348

The embossed inscription with the Medici emblem running around the bell tells us that this work was also commissioned by Cosimo dei Medici at the time of the rebuilding of the church. The frieze with dancing putti is similar to that on the cantoria which Donatello sculpted for the Duomo in 1439, again suggesting that it was made at that time and came from the same workshop. The bell later became the symbol of the revolt against the Medici family when on 6 April 1498 it rang out to sound the alarm and rally the populace to the defence of Savonarola who was beseiged in the monastery. Following Savonarola's death, the bell was ignominiously sent to San Salvatore al Monte. Julius II had it brought back to San Marco in 1501.

CHAPTER HOUSE

The bell stands in front of the Chapter House, which overlooks the cloister and is dominated by the great *Crucifixion* by Fra Angelico. The architectural structure of the Chapter House dates from the medieval monastic settlement. The emblematic figure of St Dominic with the rule in one hand and the discipline in the other, frescoed by Angelico above the door – today detached and attested to *in loco* by the light sinopia on the wall – sums up the function of this room, which was used by the monastic authorities for meetings in which the problems and decisions of the community were discussed and possible revocations of the rule were judged.

FRA ANGELICO (c 1395 - 1455)
Crucifixion with Saints
550x950 cm, fresco

The fresco, which was completed by 1442, more than being a description of
the event, is an object of meditation and collective reflection.

The artist ranges his monumental figures against a broad background, which
was originally blue (before the loss of the azurite pigment and the
uncovering of the grey and red preparatory ground) and on bare ground
devoid of any naturalistic characterization, thus heightening the tragic
intensity of the event. Alongside the historical figures (the Virgin, the Maries
and St John) are the saints associated with the Medici family, the monastery
and Florence (Cosmas and Damian, Lawrence, Mark, John the Baptist), the
Fathers of the Church and the founding saints of the main religious orders
(Dominic, Ambrose, Augustine, Benedict, Romuald, Thomas, Jerome,
Francis, Bernard, Giovanni Gualberto and Peter Martyr).

In the decorative fascia we see the pelican (the symbol of Christ), the
prophets and the Eritrean Sibyl; in the lower medallions St Dominic and the
most illustrious men of the Church.

MATTEO ROSSELLI (1578 - 1650)
Death of St Antonino
234x432 cm, fresco

This lunette, which ends the cycle of the saint's life, was executed in 1626, seventy years before those painted by Pier Dandini which precede it. Matteo Rosselli received his training at the school of Pagani and Passignano, whom he followed during a brief stay in Rome. He was highly esteemed in Florence where he executed important commissions and within a short time became an established artist, drawing to his circle painters like Furini, Vignali and Giovanni di San Giovanni. In this lunette he combined references to Poccetti's compositional prototypes with warmer, more intense colours and innovative light effects.

LAVATORIUM

After completing the round of the cloister, we now enter the door surmounted by Angelico's lunette with the *Pietà* which leads into the anteroom of the Great Refectory. This room was reserved for the lavatorium, which was usually made of stone or marble (no trace of which remains), and in which according to custom the monks ritually purified themselves before preparing to eat.

The room now contains various detached frescoes and sinopia from the cloister, a Della Robbia relief and, temporarily, two panels by Fra Angelico and two paintings by Paolo Uccello, who was one of Angelico's contemporaries yet a very different interpreter of the Renaissance.

PAOLO UCCELLO (1397 - 1475)
Madonna and Child
90x102 cm, detached fresco, Comune dep. inv. no. 192

The fresco, which was found in the house of Antonia di Giovanni del Beccuto, Paolo Uccello's mother, was saved in the course of the 19th-century demolition of Florence's old city centre. It was recognized as one of the painter's early works, close to the *Annunciation* of the Ashmolean Museum in Oxford and is therefore datable to the 1420s. Executed at the same time as Angelico's early works, the fresco reveals clearly how the common late-Gothic background of the two artists was developed by this painter with totally divergent results.

FRA ANGELICO (c 1395 - 1455)
St John the Baptist and St Benedict
St Francis and St Honofrius
170x79 cm, wood

The most widely (although not universally) accepted hypothesis is that the two panels were originally part of one of the two lost triptychs of the Carthusian monastery of Galluzzo which are mentioned by Vasari. The central part of the triptych may have been the *Virgin and Child and the Holy Trinity*, now in the Pilgrims' Hospice, which the panels resemble stylistically and to which they correspond chronologically.

Although severely damaged in the past by poor restoration the paintings are still important representative works of the artist's little-known early period.

ANDREA DELLA ROBBIA (1435 - 1525)
Madonna in Adoration of the Child
136x80 cm, glazed terracotta

The theme of the Adoration is one of the most popular of those adopted by the sculptor for the compositions he created around the 1480s and reproduced for long after in order to satisfy the increasing demand for devotional objects used for private worship. This tabernacle, of unknown provenance, bearing the coat of arms of the marriage between Brunazio Compagni and Antonietta Landi in 1485, is a variant of the prototype of the so-called *Madonna of the Lilies*, today at the National Gallery in Washington.

GREAT REFECTORY

The Lavatorium leads into the Fra Bartolomeo Room (on the left), and into the Great Refectory (on the right), a splendid medieval room with ribbed vaulting over which Michelozzo built the first dormitory on the first floor. It is dominated by the magnificent fresco with the *Miraculous Supper of St Dominic* painted by Giovanni Antonio Sogliani in 1536. It now houses a gallery of devotional paintings brought here from suppressed monasteries, mostly 16th century and linked to the culture of Fra Bartolomeo, but also of later date.

GIOVANNI ANTONIO SOGLIANI (1492 - 1544)
Miraculous Supper of St Dominic
500x792 cm, fresco

The fresco, initialled and dated 1536, shows a highly unusual iconography which may have been suggested to Sogliani by the Dominicans themselves after they had refused the first subject he had presented. It combines the theme of the Crucifixion with the Virgin, St John, St Antonino, and St Catherine of Siena, common in refectories of the 14th century, with that of the Last Supper, the subject which prevailed in the 15th century, although the latter has been transformed here into the representation of the *Miraculous Supper of St Dominic*, an episode in the saint's life with a clearly symbolic and religious significance for the community. The composition is classical, though sensitive in its realistic portrayal of some of the faces – note the figure of Molletti, the young novice dressed in white, who financed the painting of the fresco. The artist re-elaborates and fuses 15th-century themes with more modern ones deriving from Fra Bartolomeo, Albertinelli and Andrea del Sarto with a measured and melancholy simplicity that reminds us of Savonarola.

GIOVANNI ANTONIO SOGLIANI (1492 - 1544)
The Virgin Gives the Girdle to St Thomas
218x197 cm, wood, inv. 1890 no. 8642

Dated 1521 on the tomb, this altarpiece belongs to the artist's earliest known period when, although already a master in his own right, he was still strongly influenced by Lorenzo Credi, whose academic formality, typical of his early works, can be seen in some of the figures and in the layout of the composition. But we can also see an attempt to express a religious piety in the style of Fra Bartolomeo and a chiaroscural resonance reminiscent of Andrea del Sarto.

PLAUTILLA NELLI (1523 - 1588)
Lamentation over the Deposed Christ
288x192 cm, wood, inv. 1890 no. 3490

The painting came from the church of the convent of Santa Caterina of Siena (also in Piazza San Marco), of which Sister Plautilla was the Mother Superior.

This work, painted with great devotion, has an iconographical theme that was popular with Fra Bartolomeo and Fra Paolino, of whom the artist was a pupil, enriched with stylistic and typological details in the style of northern European engravings.

Plautilla Nelli was a painter highly admired by Vasari, and despite being little known is one of the few female artists whose paintings and miniatures have survived to this day.

LORENZO LIPPI (1606 - 1665)
Crucifixion with the Virgin, St John and Mary Magdalen
370x190 cm, canvas, inv. 1890 no. 2115

The painting belongs to the artist's maturity when, no longer under the influence of Matteo Rosselli, he was intensely attracted to the Counter-reformation art of Santi di Tito, which was inspired by an adherence to realism. The holy drama is characterized by a measured composure; the courtly models of the 16th century are made more familiar and more accessible to worship by ordinary people, with a certain indulgence in formal softness. The work comes from the Compagnia della Scala; the artist, who had belonged to it, donated it to the company in 1647.

F I L I P P O   T A R C H I A N I   (1576 – 1645)
Agony in the Garden
283x211 cm, canvas, inv. 1890 no. 4661

The lavish colour and exuberant naturalism of the canvas (of unknown provenance) reveals the strong influence on this highly talented artist of Empoli, the leading exponent of the Florentine naturalistic reform at the beginning of the 17th century. After a stay in Rome Tarchiani enriched his art with experimental light effects not unreminiscent of Caravaggio.

Fra Bartolomeo Room

This room, formerly used as the monastery's kitchen, today houses a collection of the works of Fra Bartolomeo, the second Dominican friar and painter of great importance who lived in San Marco and had his workshop here from the early years of the 16th century until his death in 1517. Developing and enlarging the space and harmony of 15th-century classicism, Fra Bartolomeo developed a style that drew on a classicism which was more monumental and vibrant in colour and chiaroscuro and which proved to be of great inspiration to Raphael.

Fra Bartolomeo (1472 - 1517)
St Mary Magdalen
47x35 cm, fresco on tile, inv. 1890 no. 8512

This painting, executed in fresco on the unusual support of a tile, was certainly inserted into the wall originally. It is part of a series with an *Ecce Homo* and *Saints*, displayed in this same room, and comes from the Dominican monastery of the Maddalena at Caldine near Fiesole where Fra Bartolomeo, who stayed there on several occasions and died in 1517, left other works of great intensity. The luminous, delicate colour of this tile would suggest that both it and the others were painted at about the same time as the *Christ and Pilgrims on the Road to Emmaus*, a detached fresco now in Savonarola's cell, executed around 1506.

F R A B A R T O L O M E O (1472 - 1517)
and M A R I O T T O A L B E R T I N E L L I (1474 - 1515)
Last Judgement
360x375 cm, detached fresco, inv. 1890 no. 3211

The fresco was commissioned to Fra Bartolomeo in 1499 by Gerozzo
Dini, representative of the hospital of Santa Maria Nuova, for his mother's
tomb in the Chiostro delle Ossa of the same hospital. The artist executed
only the upper part of the painting, abandoning the work after a year in
order to embrace a religious life. The fresco was finished by Mariotto
Albertinelli, his workshop assistant, in 1501. The work deteriorated rapidly
and was "detached" together with the wall on which it was painted and
divided into nine pieces before 1657, the year in which the cloister was
demolished. Successive restorations sought to prevent further deterioration,
which was arrested only after a recent intervention that involved
transferring the pictorial surface onto a suitably inert support. Despite its
extremely patchy state of conservation we can still appreciate the spatial
grandiosity of the composition, with its classical structure, which Raphael
used as a model when he painted the *Disputa* in Rome in 1509.

Fʀᴀ Bᴀʀᴛᴏʟᴏᴍᴇᴏ
Madonna and Child with St Anne and Other Saints
444x305 cm, wood, inv. 1890 no. 1574

This work, otherwise known as the "Signoria Altarpiece", was commissioned to the artist in 1510 by Pier Soderini, gonfalonier of the republic, for the new Sala del Consiglio in Palazzo Vecchio, seat of the republican parliament after the exile of the Medici in 1494. Its purpose, also present in the frescoes painted by Leonardo and Michelangelo, was to glorify Florence as a free, democratic city. The iconography is that of a 'Sacra Conversazione' of ten saints on the theme of the Immaculate Conception, represented by St Anne, the Virgin and the Child. According to Vasari the painting depicts all the patron saints of Florence and those of the days on which the city had won victories, as well as the artist's self-portrait (second from left). In 1513 the painting was left unfinished in the preparatory state in which we see it today because the fall of the Florentine republic in 1512 had invalidated its function.

BALDOVINETTI ROOM

This room is adjacent to the old kitchen (now the Fra Bartolomeo Room). The old stone lavatorium inserted into the wall is surviving evidence of its original use as a service room, connected to the old cellars and a mezzanine storeroom. Today it is dedicated to Alesso Baldovinetti, author of the standard with *Christ on the Cross Adored by St Antonino*, a versatile painter who drew on Domenico Veneziano and Fra Angelico (whose assistant he was) before adopting a more linear style in the manner of artists like Andrea del Castagno and Antonio Pollaiolo. Today the room contains a small collection of works by artists from central Italy, who with varying intensity registered the influence of Angelico in their cultural formation.

Attr. to ALESSO BALDOVINETTI (1425 - 1499)
Christ on the Cross Adored by St Antonino
276x147 cm, canvas, San Marco inv. no. 277

The canvas was originally rectangular in form and intended as a processional standard before being placed in its beautiful late 15th-century arched frame. Although the sources assigned it to Piero or Antonio del Pollaiolo, it was later attributed (not universally) to Baldovinetti and dated to the 1470s because of similarities with the *Holy Trinity* of the Galleria dell'Accademia. The delicate line of cypress trees receding into the distance recalls Angelico, while the crisp drapery and nervous outline point to the influence of Andrea del Castagno.

Attr. to B A R T O L O M E O   C A P O R A L I (1420 – before 1505)
Madonna and Child with Four Angels
79x55 cm, wood, inv. 1890 no. 3250

Generally considered to be an early work by Caporali, this panel is stylistically
close to the San Domenico altarpiece in Perugia painted with Bonfigli in 1467.
Caporali's artistic style is a refined re-statement of Angelico's models. The artist,
however, places more emphasis on the decorative aspects of narration, without
fully grasping the meaning of the Renaissance renewal.

B E N O Z Z O   G O Z Z O L I (1420/25 - 1497)
**The Mystic Marriage of St Catherine, Christ in the Sepulchre with St
John and Mary Magdalen, St Anthony Abbot and St Benedict**
21x221 cm, wood, inv. 1890 no. 886

This is the only painting in the Museum by this prolific artist who trained at the
school of Fra Angelico in San Marco. It was originally in Santa Croce where it
formed the predella of an as yet unidentified altarpiece.
Stylistically close to the frescoes in the Medici Chapel painted in 1458-59, the
scene is painted with a delicate mastery revealing Gozzoli's technical skill and the
influence of Angelico, though with more superficial and descriptive modes.

Our visit of the Museum continues into the small 15th-century Chiostro della Spesa, which in the 17th century was crowned by a small loggia, and from here to the Foresteria (guest rooms) and Small Refectory until we come to the stairway that leads to the first floor. In the winter months, when the cloister is closed, the upper floor is reached by returning to the Cloister of St Antonino and entering the corridor leading through to the large Cloister of St Dominic (today used by the friars) where there is a precious wooden *Crucifix* by Baccio da Montelupo. Here we find the stairs leading up to the first floor, leaving on our left the Small Refectory with Ghirlandaio's *Last Supper* which we shall visit at the end of our tour of the first floor.

BACCIO DA MONTELUPO (1469 - 1533)
Crucifix
height 170 cm, carved and painted wood, San Marco inv. no. 278

A record of payment dates this painting 1496. It was originally in the choir of the church and was mentioned and admired by Vasari. The work is characterized by its harmonious proportions and soft, moulded forms. The formal purity is barely disturbed by the realistic details – the thin, parched lips of death and the gaping wounds from which blood flows. The composition is true to the Savonarolian concept of art, the sole function of which was didactic, the aim being to educate the people and direct them towards religion and prayer.

first floor
THE DORMITORIES

At the top of the stairs the visitor is greeted by the famous *Annunciation* which Fra Angelico painted on the wall of one of the two corridors of the dormitories. The dormitories surround the Cloister of St Antonino on three sides, and while two of them have cells along both sides of the corridor, the third, overlooking Piazza San Marco, has cells only along the inner side. Except for the three rooms used as cells by Savonarola at the head of the third corridor, all the other forty-three cells are frescoed with scenes from the life of Christ; some of these scenes, like the Crucifixion, are repeated with some variation. The stories are not arranged in chronological order, being intended for the private contemplation of the friars who inhabited the cells. There are also three frescoes on the walls of the corridors which were intended for the communal devotion of the friars at the various times and in the ways forseen by the Dominican rule. Fra Angelico was artistically responsible for the entire cycle of paintings, which were for the most part executed between 1438 and 1445 and may have been completed after an interruption in 1451-52. The frescoes are the largest and most homogeneous nucleus of Angelico's artistic production, executed with the help of assistants, including Benozzo Gozzoli.

F R A   A N G E L I C O (c 1395 – 1455)
Annunciation
230x297 cm, fresco

This composition, which greets the visitor at the entrance to the dormitory, is one of Angelico's most famous works. The recent restoration has brought to light the clearness of the architectural setting – evidently inspired by Michelozzo's

cloister on the ground floor – as well as the moulding of the Virgin's blue cloak, the vividness and luminosity of the colours and the shimmer of the gold. As a result the scene has regained the effect of perspective created by the different planes formed by the window, the grass and the floor of the loggia.

The date of the work is uncertain, oscillating between the first period of the artist's work at San Marco in around 1440 and a probable second period after his return from Rome in around 1450.

FRA ANGELICO (c 1395 – 1455)
Christ on the Cross Adored by St Dominic
237x125 cm, fresco

The fresco is one of the three situated in communal areas of the dormitory. In the very place which marked the entry into nocturnal meditation, it shows the fundamental image of Dominican worship, and one we have already encountered in the cloister. Devoid here of even the naturalistic touch of the sky in the background, and surrounded by the stylized frame, it rather has the appearance of a symbolic frontispiece to the monastic rule.

First Corridor

The cell opposite the fresco with *Christ on the Cross Adored by St Dominic* marks the beginning of the first dormitory which Michelozzo built in 1437 by raising the medieval refectory. It comprises twenty cells frescoed from 1438 by Fra Angelico, with scenes relating to the life, death and resurrection of Christ, without any chronological order in the sequence of the episodes depicted. The cells situated on this side are almost completely the work of Angelico, with extremely limited contributions on the part of assistants, and represent some of the painter' highest achievements.

Cell 1
FRA ANGELICO (c 1395 – 1455)
Noli Me Tangere
166x125 cm, fresco

In this work we can clearly see how Angelico used only the different tonalities of colour to create the sculptural quality of the forms. The figure of Mary Magdalen, a bright mass of colour against the natural landscape of the background, reaches forward to embrace the risen Christ, who, swathed in light, appears before her in the guise of a gardener.

Cell 2
FRA ANGELICO
Lamentation over the Deposed Christ
184x152 cm, fresco

The iconography of the scene resembles that of the panel in Santa Maria della
Croce al Tempio. The expression and emotional force of the image, however,
derive from the daring and refined combination of colours. The surreal
atmosphere thus created makes the scene appear more like a vision seen by
St Dominic, who is depicted in contemplation at the side.

Cell 3
FRA ANGELICO (c 1395 - 1455)
Annunciation
176x148 cm, fresco

The setting here is also a cloister, although it is very different from the one in the famous *Annunciation* at the top of the stairs. The image here is intended for private meditation by the monks; the figure of St Peter Martyr praying at the side acts as mediator for the holy vision. The scene is devoid of any narrative or decorative element; the architectural setting is limited by the receding vaults of the cloister, but the two figures appear to stand in an abstract space, emphasized by the multiple curves of the vaults which frame them, an effect that was quite avant-garde for the time. There is no gold and the precious and costly azurite which should have coloured the green drawing (contrasting with the chiaroscural red) of the Virgin's robe, is missing and indeed may never have been applied.

Cell 4
FRA ANGELICO
Crucifixion with the Virgin and Saints John, Dominic and Jerome
178x150 cm, fresco

This is the first of the numerous Crucifixions that we shall see in the cells. The artist has placed the Crucifix in the centre of the composition, whose spatial arrangement is rigorously constructed. The cross stands against a black background – an unusual colour, faithful to the description of the Scriptures, often used by Angelico for this scene – which contrasts dramatically with the composed grief of the onlookers: on the left the real witnesses of the event; on the right two of the historical ones.

Cell 5
FRA ANGELICO (c 1395 - 1455) and assistant
Nativity
177x148 cm, fresco

Some scholars claim that this fresco, whose compositional scheme is the same as that of one of the panels of the Silver Cabinet (Pilgrims' Hospice), was not executed entirely by Angelico. Although the master was certainly responsible for the conception of the work, the identification of the different *giornate* (workdays) which became visible after the restoration of the frescoes made it possible to distinguish the areas materially painted by him, such as the area with the extremely delicate figure of the Child, from those areas executed often less skilfully by his assistants, like that with the angels above.

Cell 6
F R A   A N G E L I C O
Transfiguration
181x152 cm, fresco

The fresco in this cell represents the most spectacular example of Angelico's mastery of colour. The scene is dominated by the figure of Christ standing in the form of a cross and bathed in radiant light created by a subtle play of various shades of white. In a ring around him, blinded by the vision, are the disciples Peter, James and John, then the Virgin and St Dominic, and finally Moses and Elijah.

Cell 7
FRA ANGELICO (c 1395 - 1455)
The Mocking of Christ with the Virgin and St Dominic
187x151 cm, fresco

The raised, central figure of Christ is blindfolded; he holds the reed and the globe,
symbols of power given to him mockingly by his persecutors, and is surrounded
by images of derision typical of medieval iconography: the head of a ruffian who
spits at him, hands that slap him and hands holding a reed to beat him. Below,
absorbed in meditation, are the Virgin and the wonderfully expressive figure
of St Dominic.

Cell 8
FRA ANGELICO
Maries at the Sepulchre
181x151 cm, fresco

The most intense part of the fresco is again the figure of St Dominic on the left, seen in profile in blessed contemplation, or rather imagination, of the open tomb discovered by the holy women. The light surrounding him, isolating him from the rest of the scene, emphasizes his particular state of grace. The Virgin Mary is caught in a moment of bewilderment before the empty tomb while the other two holy women form a painted group of great elegance. The latter, however, lack the intensity of expression typical of Angelico, suggesting that they are probably the work of an assistant.

Cell 9
FRA ANGELICO (c 1395 - 1455)
Coronation of the Virgin
171x151 cm, fresco

In this work Angelico's mastery of colour uses all the varying shades of white to create clothes, figures and light. The composition's arrangement in concentric circles is reminiscent of medieval theological theory: the upper circle with Christ and the Virgin is flooded with brilliant light and surrounded by spheres of white, green and pink light created by liquidy brushstrokes of transparent colour. In the lower circle are representatives of the Christian church: Saints Thomas, Benedict, Dominic, Francis, Peter Martyr and Mark.

Cell 10
FRA ANGELICO
Presentation in the Temple
171x116 cm, fresco

Recent restoration has brought to light, beneath an overpainting of red tempera, the splendid Renaissance niche in the background, which was unfortunately damaged in the past at the top. Here, some traces of the preparatory charcoal drawing are visible on the first layer of plaster. This is one of the most intensely poetic of all the scenes painted in the cells.

Cell 11
FRA ANGELICO (c 1395 - 1455) and assistant
Madonna Enthroned between Saints Zenobius and Thomas
179x150 cm, fresco

This cell, joined to the preceding one by an arch which was at some time walled up, may have been used by the head of the novices who inhabited the cells of the second dormitory. The figure of St Zenobius, on the left, shows the unmistakable mastery of Angelico in the purity of the brushstrokes and in the transparent colours, whereas the other figures have a less confident line that can be attributed to the hand of an assistant.

SECOND CORRIDOR

The second corridor, in addition to the three rooms at the end used by Savonarola, consists of only seven cells on the inner side (from 15 to 22). Michelozzzo built the dormitory by raising the walls of the medieval structure below, whose existence has been confirmed by the fragments of 14th-century wall painting recently discovered on both longitudinal walls, in the portion between the floor and the impost of the underlying vaults. The oldest fragment, dating from the early 14th century, is at cell 17 and consists of a lunette with *Saints Anthony Abbot and Benedict (*or *Silvestro Guzzolini)*; it refers, therefore, to the foundation of the congregation of Silvestrine monks, the monastery's first inhabitants.

Cells 15-21
Attr. to B E N O Z Z O   G O Z Z O L I (1420/25 - 1497)
Christ on the Cross Adored by St Dominic
frescos

The cells in this corridor were reserved for novices. The depiction of St Dominic praying at the foot of the cross was intended to provide religious inspiration and is repeated in each cell with only slight variations. In each fresco we see St Dominic in different attitudes of prayer and contemplation – ecstasy, compunction, penitence and others – according to the indications of Dominican prayer ritual laid down by St Dominic himself. In cell 21 Angelico's compositional idea is translated into a more graphic and descriptive representation that is uncharacteristic of the master and may therefore be by Gozzoli.

Savonarola's Cells

In the period during which he lived at San Marco and was prior from
1491 until his death he occupied three rooms at the end of the second
corridor. The first was used as a chapel, the second as a study, and the third
as a cell. Today, in addition to the relics, sacred texts and objects belonging
to the friar, there is also the tomb monument erected in his honour in
1873, in full Risorgimento spirit, by Giovanni Duprè, the portraits painted
by Fra Bartolomeo, his admirer and disciple (and author of various
detached frescoes on the walls of the chapel), and a banner painted by him
used in processions.

Fra Girolamo was born in Ferrara in 1452. He joined the Dominican
order in Bologna in 1474 and came to Florence ten years later, where he
preached violently and prophetically against the decline of traditions, the
vanity of the times, and the corruption of the Church and those who held
power. It was not long before his invective became a specific accusation
directed at the tyrannical methods adopted by the Medicean Signoria and
a rallying cry for the reconquest of freedom and republican institutions.
Savonarola's actions provoked divisions and feuds between opposing
factions, and eventually led to his capture and execution in 1498.

Fra Bartolomeo (1472 - 1517)
Portrait of Fra Girolamo Savonarola
53x37 cm, wood, inv. 1890 no. 8550

This portrait of the Ferrarese preacher, greatly admired by Vasari, was painted by
Fra Bartolomeo during the period Savonarola resided at San Marco. The image is
one of intense psychological penetration: the head is defined by a clear-cut profile,
reminiscent of 15th-century prototypes, and is totally devoid of any
environmental or descriptive background, which according to Savonarola's idea of
art was superfluous.

FLORENTINE ARTIST of the late 15th/early 16th century
Piazza della Signoria and the Martyrdom of Savonarola
100x115 cm, wood, San Marco inv. no. 477

This painting is a document of extraordinary interest not only for the historical event, which is depicted with great accuracy – the martyrdom of Savonarola and his companions who were hung and burnt at the stake in Piazza della Signoria – but also for the detailed representation of contemporary Florence, showing the remarkable brick pavement of the Piazza.

FRA BARTOLOMEO (1472 - 1517)
Portrait of Fra Girolamo Savonarola as St Peter Martyr
52x40 cm, wood, inv. 1890 no. 8522

This painting, modelled on the preceding one, was evidently executed after Savonarola's death. The iconographical association of Savonarola with St Peter of Verona, one of the first martyrs of the Dominican order, who was executed after a period of persecution, is significant.

FRA BARTOLOMEO
Christ and Pilgrims on the Road to Emmaus
103x116 cm, detached fresco

Originally above the entrance to the Foresteria (guest-quarters), the fresco was moved here at the end of the 19th century together with the other two frescoes of the *Madonna and Child*, which had been removed some time before from the monastery at Caldine. The disciple seen in profile on the right is a portrait of Niccolò Scomberg, who became prior of San Marco in 1506 after Santi Pagnini, whose portrait can be seen in the figure of the other disciple. 1506 is therefore a *post quem* for the dating of this work.

FIRST CORRIDOR (left side)

Our visit continues with the frescoes of the cells on the left-hand side of the corridor, which include scenes of the *Baptism of Christ* (cell 24), *Christ Rising from the Sepulchre* (cell 26), the *Flagellation* (cell 27) and *Christ Carrying the Cross* (cell 28), as well as various *Crucifixions*, with variations on the iconographical theme already encountered in cell 4, almost exclusively in the identity and in the pose of the Dominican saint who metaphorically witnesses the scene. The most recent view is that Fra Angelico was responsible for the overall conception of the compositions, though his direct participation in their execution was limited to a few *giornate* (workdays), their completion being left increasingly to his assistants.

Cell 22
FRA ANGELICO (c 1395 - 1455)
and assistant
Crucifixion with the Virgin in Mourning
144x81 cm, fresco

FLORENTINE PAINTER
of the late 14th century
Vir Dolorum and the Holy Monk
84x280 cm, fresco

The cell contains a *Crucifixion* similar to those painted in the cells of the novices, but here the figure of St Dominic has been replaced by that of the Virgin. Another fragmentary fresco, datable to the end of the 14th century and therefore to before the building of the dormitory, is also visible. It was discovered under the floor on the remaining part of a transversal wall that had been partially demolished in the 15th century when the vault beneath and the pavement above were constructed.

Cell 24
F R A A N G E L I C O (c 1395 – 1455) and assistant
Baptism of Christ
179x148 cm, fresco

The inventiveness of the composition, dominated by the receding landscape, the choice of an almost surreal colour palette and the idea of iridescent concentric circles accompanying the arrival of the dove certainly indicates, whoever was responsible for the actual painting, that the original idea was Angelico's. It is just as certain that the dry, stiff draughtsmanship of the figures can only be the work of an assistant.

Cell 23
FRA ANGELICO and assistant
Crucifixion with the Virgin, St Dominic and Angels
177x137 cm, fresco

Cell 25
FRA ANGELICO and assistant
Crucifixion with the Virgin, St Dominic and Mary Magdalen
176x136 cm, fresco

Cell 26
FRA ANGELICO and assistants
Christ Rising from the Sepulchre with the Virgin and St Thomas
165x142 cm, fresco

Left wall of the corridor

FRA ANGELICO (c 1395 - 1455)
Madonna and Child Enthroned with Saints Dominic, Cosmas, Damian, Mark, John the Evangelist, Thomas, Lawrence and Peter Martyr
193x273 cm, 130x273 cm (lower border), fresco and tempera

This 'Sacra Conversazione' is also known as the *Madonna of the Shadows* because of the light coming from the left (as does the real light) which causes the architecture to cast shadows. The work closely resembles the altarpieces and a recent restoration has revealed that Angelico used a similar technique of egg tempera on a fresco base for most of the composition. Although the proportions, the compositional order and the architectural form of the background wall, subdivided by fluted pilasters with Corinthian capitals, suggest an affinity with contemporary Florentine architecture, the work probably belongs to a later period after Angelico's return from Rome in 1450.

Cell 27
FRA ANGELICO
and assistants
Flagellation
165x142 cm, fresco

Cell 28
F R A   A N G E L I C O   and assistants
Christ Carrying the Cross with the Virgin and St Dominic (?)
148x131 cm, fresco

Cell 29
F R A   A N G E L I C O   and assistants
Crucifixion with the Virgin and St Peter Martyr
124x128 cm, fresco

Cell 30
F R A   A N G E L I C O   and assistants
Crucifixion with the Virgin and St Dominic
157x132 cm, fresco

The cells on the left-hand side of the dormitory, those looking onto the cloister (from 31 to 37), contain more frescoes with episodes from the life of Christ. Here, the scenes suddenly become more descriptive and the compositions more complex in their spatial structure, in the number of figures and in the details of the landscape. The style is more graphic and more vivid, revealing the increasingly distinctive hand of assistants, particularly Gozzoli, certainly in the execution of the fresco and probably also on the sinopia drawn by Angelico. It seems that Gozzoli was also responsible for the execution of a large part of the frescoes in the cells on the right-hand side of the corridor dedicated to the theme of the Crucifixion, with the exception of the fresco in the cell 42 where the refined quality suggests it was executed entirely by Angelico.

Cell 31
F R A   A N G E L I C O   (c 1395 - 1455) and assistant
Christ in Limbo
183x166 cm, fresco

Historical sources suggest that this was the cell of St Antonino, who became prior of the monastery in 1439 and later bishop of Florence. He probably inspired the theological themes of the entire cycle. The inspiration for this scene is Angelico's but the execution of the painting, which is more descriptive and more detailed, is probably the work of assistants whose role is increasingly evident in the frescoes of this corridor.

Cells 32 and 32a
FRA ANGELICO
and assistants
**Sermon on the Mount
Temptation of Christ
in the Desert**
190x198 cm, fresco;
174x137 cm, incomplete fresco

Cells 33 and 33a
F R A A N G E L I C O
(c 1395 - 1455)
and assistant
The Betrayal of Judas
Entry into Jerusalem
182x181 cm, fresco;
163x54 cm, incomplete fresco

Cell 34
F R A A N G E L I C O and
B E N O Z Z O G O Z Z O L I
(1420/25 - 1497)
Agony in the Garden
177x147 cm, fresco

This fresco, in which a daring spatial
division allows the simultaneous
representation of physically distant
episodes, shows how the ingenious
idea of the master is realized with
the descriptive style and delicate
colours typical of Gozzoli.

Cell 35
F R A A N G E L I C O
and assistants
Institution of the Eucharist
186x234 cm, fresco

Cell 36
FRA ANGELICO (c 1395 – 1455) and assistants
Christ nailed to the Cross
169x134 cm, fresco

Cell 37
FRA ANGELICO and assistants
**Crucifixion with St John the Evangelist, the Virgin, St Dominic
and St Thomas**
213x165 cm, fresco

Cell 38
FRA ANGELICO
and BENOZZO GOZZOLI (1420/25 – 1497)
Crucifixion with the Virgin and Saints Cosmas, John and Peter Martyr
152x112 cm, fresco

Cell 39
F R A A N G E L I C O and B E N O Z Z O G O Z Z O L I
Adoration of the Magi
175x357 cm, 86x60 cm (tabernacle), fresco

Cells 38 and 39 are the rooms which Cosimo had set aside in the monastery for
his own private meditation and in which Pope Eugenius IV was also
accommodated on the night of Epiphany in 1443 when he was present at the
consecration of the new church of San Marco. The end wall of the second cell is
entirely taken up by the large fresco of the *Adoration of the Magi*, in which a
striking tabernacle with the *Dead Christ* is inserted, whose execution, certainly on
Angelico's design, is generally agreed to be by Gozzoli. The courtly atmosphere of
the rich setting contrasts with the simplicity of the works in the other cells. The
extravagant fashions of some of the costumes suggest that the artist drew
inspiration for the work from the gathering of people at the Council of
Florence in 1439.

Cell 40
F R A   A N G E L I C O   (c 1395 – 1455) and assistant
Crucifixion
178x181 cm, fresco

Cell 41
F R A   A N G E L I C O   and assistant
Crucifixion
181x160 cm, fresco

Cell 43
F R A   A N G E L I C O   and assistant
Crucifixion with the Virgin, St John, Mary Magdalen and St Dominic
169x138 cm, fresco

Cell 42
FRA ANGELICO
**Crucifixion with Saints Mark (?), Dominic (?), Longinus, Martha
and Mary**
196x199 cm, fresco

The theme of the Crucifixion is depicted with iconographical variations in many
of the cells but never with such dramatic force as here. The absence of any
environmental setting lends emphasis to the poses of the figures, which are
portrayed as masses of colour and light against an abstract background. Such
refinement and compositional synthesis indicate that the fresco was almost
certainly painted by Angelico towards the end of his work in the cells.

Library

The entrance to the library is opposite the large window, built in the 17th century and overlooking the cloister, and beyond the vestibule, where a stone tablet records Savonarola's capture here on the night of 8 July 1498. Stripped of its original furnishings the room appears even more solemn, its basilical structure with a nave and two side aisles in marked contrast with the absolute simplicity and even size of the dormitory cells, underlining the importance which this place set aside for study and for the conservation of books must have had in the new monastery. The precious collection of classical texts belonging to the humanist scholar Niccolò Niccoli, which Cosimo de' Medici acquired for the monastery, has been removed; today the library houses an important collection of illuminated choirbooks and psalters of various period and provenance, which are displayed in rotation.

FLORENTINE MINIATURIST (late 13th century)
Madonna and Child Enthroned
initial S on c. 16r., Gradual G (ms. 562), parchment

This choirbook comes from the monastery of San Jacopo di Ripoli. Together
with the one marked 561, it is one of the oldest in the Museum's possession. The
initials are illuminated with the simple elegance typical of 13th-century book
decoration, characterized by the use of a limited range of bright colours. In the
decorated initials, like the one illustrated here, we can admire the work of an artist
of Florentine cultural background – the influence of the *Madonna della Scarsella* in
the Baptistery being evident – who elaborated Byzantine models in the style of
contemporary Cimabuesque painting and the Bolognese miniaturist school.

MASTER OF THE DOMINICAN PORTRAITS
(first half of the 14th century)
The Perseverance of Job
initial S on c. 13v, Antiphonary D (ms. 564), parchment

This antiphonary comes from the monastery of Santa Maria Novella, of which the
Museum houses a precious series of choirbooks. It is the work of a miniaturist and
painter who was extremely active in Florence in the first half of the 14th century,
open to the influence of Bernardo Daddi and also of Jacopo del Casentino, with
whom he may even have collaborated in the illustration of this choirbook.
Manuscript decoration became more elaborate in the 14th century with the
appearance of gold and with more varied plant and animal ornamental motifs; the
initials no longer house isolated figures only, but little scenes of extraordinary
expressive force.

DON SIMONE CAMALDOLESE (second half of the 14th century)
Massacre of the Innocents
initial S on c. 70r, Antiphonary T (ms. 571), parchment

This belongs to the large number of 14th-century codices which came from the
church of the Carmine. They were illuminated by the most celebrated exponent
of the famous Scuola degli Angeli, a Camaldolensian monk originally from Siena
who gave impetus to a great "scriptorium" where artists of the calibre of Lorenzo
Monaco received their training. The refined draughtsmanship and brilliant
colours in the limited space of the miniature successfully convey the
monumentality of contemporary painting, at the time dominated by the
Orcagna brothers.

BARTOLOMEO DI FRUOSINO (1366 - 1441)
Bishop St Giles and Angels
initial G on c. 35v, Antiphonary no call no. (ms. 557), parchment

This antiphonary is an example of the heights of decorative virtuosity which miniature art reached at the end of the 14th and beginning of the 15th century, in the heart of the late-Gothic period. Illuminated for Santa Maria Nuova, it bears an inscription which indicates the year of execution (1421), the calligrapher, the patron and the miniaturist. The latter, who trained as a fresco painter in the school of Agnolo Gaddi, had a long working relationship with Lorenzo Monaco whose linear exasperation he took to the limits of the grotesque.

F R A A N G E L I C O (c 1395 – 1455) and assistants
St Dominic in Glory
initial I on c. 67v, Missal no call no. (ms. 558), parchment

This missal, of unknown origin, is one of the few surviving examples of the
miniature painting which Angelico did presumably in his youth. In the numerous
illuminations with which it is decorated we find ideas and motifs that will later be
more amply developed in his large compositions on wood or plaster. Not all the
miniatures are Angelico's; those completely by his hand, characterized by an
extremely high pictorial quality, reveal a preference for the linearity and soft
plasticism of Masolino's art, typical of the painter's early activity around the 1430s.
The other miniatures, which are more calligraphic, are attributed to assistants,
including Zanobi Strozzi, to whom the entire manuscript was once assigned.

ZANOBI STROZZI (1412 - 1468) and FILIPPO DI MATTEO TORELLI (records from 1440 to 1468)
Annunciation
initial R on c. 3r, Gradual B (ms. 516), parchment

This gradual is one of the eleven choirbooks illuminated by the two artists for the monastery of San Marco, of which Fra Benedetto, Angelico's brother, was calligrapher. They were commissioned by Cosimo de' Medici between 1446 and 1454. Torelli was responsible for the execution of the decorative parts, whereas the scenes with figures were the work of Zanobi Strozzi, one of Angelico's pupils. Zanobi's artistic activity still awaits comprehensive evaluation, which could be made in the light of comparisons between these and other miniatures, the only works of his that are documented.

MONTE DI GIOVANNI (1448 – 1533)
Christ Hands Over the Keys to St Peter
c. 3v, Psalter no call no. (ms. 542), parchment

The full-page illumination, illustrated here, adorns the *incipit* of a psalter illuminated in 1514–15 by Monte together with Boccardino the Elder, who was responsible for the remaining miniatures of the codex. It was done for the Badia Fiorentina, whose emblem runs along the bottom. Monte di Giovanni, who with his brother Gherardo ran a thriving workshop in Florence, introduced various innovations in the field of miniature painting, including the tendency to reduce the friezes in favour of a greater emphasis on the figures and scenes, which were classically framed with medallions or panels separated by jewel motifs.

SMALL REFECTORY

At the bottom of the stairs we turn right and enter the Small Refectory which was used by guests. This room is also named after Ghirlandaio, from the *Last Supper* frescoed on one wall. Domenico Ghirlandaio was the founder of one of the most flourishing Florentine workshops of the last decades of the 15th century, where his brothers also worked. He trained in the workshop of Verrocchio, where his fellow pupils were Perugino, Botticelli and Leonardo. Not being part of the intellectual and artistic circle that revolved around the Medici family, Ghirlandaio developed an art which aimed at the true, harmonious representation of the life and society of his time, every aspect of which was captured – from portraits and landscapes and interiors to costumes. It was a style of painting that won the favour of wealthy Florentine families, who commissioned him important wall paintings in churches like Santa Trinita and Santa Maria Novella.

ANDREA DELLA ROBBIA (1435 - 1525)
Pietà
245x188 cm, glazed terracotta

The lunette is surrounded by a beautiful frame with a garland of fruit, pine cones and flowers typical of the Robbian style. It contains the representation of Christ's deposition from the cross, his body lying in the lap of the Virgin and supported by St John and by Mary Magdalen. It is a devotional work datable to around 1510. The inscription on the base inviting the wayfarer to stop and reflect on Christ's suffering is justified by the provenance of the work from a tabernacle situated somewhere outside Florence.

DOMENICO GHIRLANDAIO (1449 - 1494)
Last Supper
420x780 cm, fresco

This is one of the four frescoes of this subject – of which the most famous is the one in Ognissanti – which Ghirlandaio painted in Florence and its surroundings between about 1476 and 1480 (the probable dating for this one of San Marco), according to the established practice from the middle of the century of decorating monastic refectories with a Last Supper instead of a Crucifixion. Ghirlandaio's compositions are apparently similar, although the painter adapted the

compositional scheme of each one to the architectural characteristics of the room. Here, conditioned by the square plan and limited depth of the room, he painted the table and bench in perspective in order to increase the depth of the scene, with a background consisting of an open sky full of plants and animals which satisfied the contemporary taste for realism and at the same time the requirements of Christian symbology. The cat near Judas, in fact, is a diabolical animal, the peacock and the pheasant are symbols of the Resurrection, the ducks are heavenly symbols, the cypress tree is a symbol of death, the palm of martyrdom, the lilies of purity and the roses of the blood of martyrdom.

Foresteria

Beyond the Small Refectory, and passing on our left a view of the 15th-century Cloister of St Dominic decorated with the stories of St Dominic, today used by the Dominican friars, we come to the Foresteria, the old guest-quarters. This consists of a gallery and six rooms which contain most of the architectural, sculptural and pictorial fragments saved from the late 19th-century demolition of the buildings in the old centre of Florence. Above the entrance doors of the rooms eight lunettes have been frescoed with Dominican saints, five of them by Fra Bartolomeo and three by an unknown 18th-century painter.

ANDREA DI NOFRI (1387/88 – documented in 1451)
Doorway
463x329x40 cm, pietra serena, inv. 1925 no. 47

The doorway, carved in 1414 and painted in 1430 by Piero di Lorenzo, which comes from the residence of the Arte dei Rigattieri, Linaioli e Sarti, the same one of the great tabernacle painted by Angelico (today in the Pilgrim's Hospice), is one of the architectural exhibits that was saved after the demolition of the old centre of Florence in the 1890s. The shields on the lintel are, from left to right, the 'Rigattieri', the Captain of the People, the Florentine Church, the Florentine Republic, the Guelph Party and again the 'Rigattieri'.

FLORENTINE WORKMANSHIP of the 16th century
Fragment of Architrave
36x92 cm, pietra serena, inv. 1925 no. 75

This is a fragment of the architrave of a door from the Jewish temple of the Ghetto. It bears a fragmentary inscription in Hebrew: THIS IS THE DOOR OF THE LORD.

FLORENTINE WORKMANSHIP of the 13th century
Mullioned Window
280x146 cm, stone, terracotta and marble, inv. 1925 no. 38

The window is made up of two arches inscribed within a third larger round arch in brick, resting on a slender marble column with a leaf ornament on the capital. It dates from the 13th century and both the form and material used indicate the influence of the Lombard style. It comes from the demolished part of the "Vescovado Vecchio" (the old Bishop's Palace).

FRA BARTOLOMEO (1472 - 1517)
St Dominic
74x120 cm, fresco

This is one of the portraits of St Dominic painted by Fra Bartolomeo probably in about 1510-11 above the doors of the rooms in the Foresteria. There is a similarity between the forceful figure of the saint in the way it seems to stand out from the niche and the frescoes by Angelico above the doors in the Cloister of St Antonino, but the expressiveness of the works is quite different.

CLOISTER OF THE SILVESTRINE MONKS

From a small room of the Foresteria we enter the old Corte del Granaio, which was originally used for the storage of food, and where today we find other architectural fragments from the old city centre. From here we enter the last remaining vestige of the medieval monastic complex, the 14th-century Cloister of the Silvestrine Monks, which contains a collection of tomb inscriptions and coats of arms, mostly from the 14th and 15th century, removed from the church of San Pancrazio in 1883.

FLORENTINE SCULPTOR of the 13th century
Carved Panel with Family Coat of Arms
83x56 cm, pietra forte, inv. 1879 no. 259
dated 1276

THE CHURCH OF SAN MARCO

Next to the Museum is the church of San Marco, founded by Silvestrine monks in 1299. Access from it to the monastery was originally through a door leading into the Cloister of St Antonino. The church's present layout and appearance are the result of the numerous transformations which the building underwent over the centuries until the 18th, the period to which the present facade dates (1777-78). The facade, designed in two orders and elegantly divided by pilaster strips, is adorned at the bottom with the statues of *St Dominic* and *St Vincent* by Agostino Nobili and Giovan Battista Capezzuoli, above with the relief of *St Antonino's Entry into Florence as Archbishop* (also by Nobili), and in the frontispiece of the door with the winged lion between angels, the symbol of St Mark, by Capezzuoli. The original Latin cross structure was modified as early as 1438 by Michelozzo, who added a semi-octagonal apse and probably demolished the right arm of the transept to create space for the monastery's cloister. The transformation of the left arm of the transept into the Chapel of St Antonino (1579-89) on a design by Giambologna (who was also responsible for the altars of the nave in 1590-94) and the building of the Serragli Chapel, or Chapel of the Holy Sacrament, on a design by Cigoli and Santi di Tito, date from the end of the 16th century.

In the last decades of the 17th century Pier Francesco Silvani began the transformation of the presbyterial area. This ended in 1712 with the building of the cupola above the choir – frescoed in 1717 by Alessandro Gherardini with the *Glory of St Mary Magdalen* – and the execution of the two great wall paintings with the *Adoration of the Magi* and the *Wedding at Cana* by Ignazio Parrocel (1712).

The late-Baroque decoration of the church was completed in 1679 with the building of the carved coffered ceiling – which now conceals the splendid original trussed roof – in which a canvas with the *Assumption of the Virgin* painted by Giovanni Antonio Pucci, the pupil of Gabbiani, was inserted in 1725.

Beginning our visit of the church on the right side, we see in the alcove of the altar in the counterfacade one of the few surviving fragments of the church's 14th-century mural decoration. This is a fresco with the *Annunciation*, a replica of the one painted in the church of Santissima Annunziata, which, as the inscription

above:
Florentine Painter of the 14th Century, Annunciation.

right:
Mosaic of the 8th Century with Madonna in Glory and Saints Dominic and Raimond frescoed in the 17th Century.

page 124
Overall View of the Salviati Chapel.

page 125
Domenico Cresti called Il Passignano, The Transfer of St Anonino's Body.

under the painting reads, was commissioned in the second half of the century by the Silvestrine monks who are portrayed on the left. Proceeding along the right-hand wall, we first come to a niche containing an *Ecce Homo*, a polychrome wooden figure carved by Jacopo Maria Foggini in 1654 for Filippo Baldinucci's family chapel, then donated to the Dominicans. This is followed by the first altar with *St Thomas and St Catherine Praying before the Crucifix* (1593), one of the most important paintings by Santi di Tito, a leading figure in the reform of Florentine painting, away from Mannerism and towards a new realism which developed at the end of the 16th century.

The second altar contains a *Sacra Conversazione*, dated 1509, the only painting remaining in the church by Fra Bartolomeo, the Dominican friar who lived at San Marco. The third altar is dominated by a large mosaic of the 8th century

representing the *Madonna in Prayer*, which was transferred here in 1609 from the
oratory of John VII in Rome. It is surrounded by the figures of *St Dominic, St
Raymond and Angels* painted in fresco in the 17th century in imitation of the
mosaic. At the following altar is a canvas by Matteo Rosselli (17th C.) with the
*Virgin, St Catherine and St Mary Magdalen Presenting the Image of St Dominic
to Two Dominican Friars*, a typical example of reformed Florentine painting.
It is set within a composite columned arch surmounted by a statue of St Zenobius,
executed by Giambologna as a companion-piece to the one in front of the Chapel
of St Antonino.
The following door, designed by Cigoli (late 16th C.), leads through a vestibule into
the Sacristy, built by Michelozzo. Today it is covered with elegant 18th-century
wardrobes in which, under the altar, is Giambologna's bronze statue of *St Antonino*.

Re-entering the church, we see in the centre of the presbytery the monumental altar in polychrome marble executed in 1697 by Romolo Tortori. This is surmounted by Fra Angelico's wooden *Crucifix*, while on the back wall is the imposing cantoria and organ front, executed, like the new choir, in 1684/85, at the same time as the wooden ceiling of the nave. Below the organ a door leads through to Michelozzo's apse, today covered with fine wardrobes dating from 1688; two portals with inlaid door-leaves survive from the architect's period. To the left of the presbytery, beneath a large arch with the statue of St Antonino, the work of Giambologna, is the left arm of the transept. This is occupied by the Salviati Chapel, dedicated to St Antonino, and the vestibule in front of it – decorated with two large wall frescoes by Domenico Cresti, known as Passignano, with the *Exposition and Transfer of St Antonino's Body* – in which there are four marble portals designed by Cigoli (1588), one of which leads into the Serragli Chapel, frescoed by Poccetti and decorated with paintings by 16th-century artists. The Salviati Chapel, built on designs by Giambologna between 1579 and 1589, with its exquisite late-Mannerist style and extraordinary harmony, is crowned by a small cupola decorated with stuccowork and frescoes. The latter are representations of the *Virtues and Stories of St Antonino* painted by Bernardino Poccetti and Alessandro Allori, who was also responsible for the central painting with the *Descent into Limbo*. On the side walls are the *Conversion of St Matthew* by Giovan Battista Naldini, the *Healing of the Leper* by Francesco Morandini, called 'Il Poppi', and niches with statues by Giambologna and Francavilla. Also by Giambologna are the bronze reliefs with *Stories from the Life of St Antonino*. Under the altar is the urn containing the intact body of St Antonino, the founder of the monastery, bishop and patron saint of Florence, who died in 1459. Proceeding along the left wall of the church, we come to a painting by Cigoli with *Heraclius Carrying the Cross* (1594), at the second altar a copy of Fra Bartolomeo's *Mystical Marriage of St Catherine* of 1512, executed by Anton Domenico Gabbiani in 1690 when the original, today at the Galleria Palatina, was sold to Grand Prince Ferdinando, and at the third altar the painting with the *Miracle of St Vincenzo Ferreri* (1593) by Passignano. In the space between the altars are pieces of the 14th and 15th-century mural paintings which adorned the wall until the construction of the 16th-century altars. A fragmentary *Last Judgement* can be made out, in which the hand of Antonio Veneziano, a late Gothic painter active at the end of the 14th century, seems recognizable, and a *Holy Martyr* figure of a little later, attributable to Bicci di Lorenzo. Also in the space between the altars are the tombstones of Giovanni Pico della Mirandola, Girolamo Benivieni and Agnolo Poliziano, famous literary figures associated with the Medici family who died in the last decade of the 15th century. At the end of the wall inside a niche is the *Manger* with almost life-size figures, including a Child dating from the 16th century. Against the counterfacade is the altar with the dazzling *Transfiguration*, dated 1596, a canvas by the Genoese artist Giovan Battista Paggi, Giambologna's friend, surmounted by an oval with the *Baptism of Christ*. Above the door, finally, is a large painted *Cross*, with the patrons at the foot of it, inspired by Giotto's large crosses, especially the one in Ognissanti, but executed later, probably around 1360 by a Florentine painter of the Orcagna circle, identified as the author of the frescoes of the Strozzi family's funerary chapel in Santa Maria Novella. Situated in the rood-screen until 1564, the year of the demolition of the church's old partition, it changed place several times before being positioned where it is today, possibly in the late-Baroque period.

Giovan Battista Paggi, Transfiguration, 1596